Mankind'
Mankind's wisdom
from Aristotle to Zimmerman

Compiled by Patty Crowe
Edited by Laura Wertz

Richer Resources Publications
Arlington, VA

Grateful acknowledgement is made to the following
individuals for the generous use of their copyrighted works:
Page 13, Bob Franke, Singer/Songwriter www.bobfranke.com
pages 11, 43 used by permission of word garden, ltd,
Salem, Oregon and maryanneradmacher.com

Reprint requests and requests for additional
copies of this book can be addressed to
Richer Resources Publications
1926 N. Woodrow Street
Arlington, Virginia 22207
or via our website at:
www.RicherResourcesPublications.com

ISBN 978-0-9776269-4-6
Library of Congress Control Number
2006923705

Printed in India by Fine Grains (India) Private Limited

To the Great Thinkers
of the Past, Present and Future

Three things cannot long be hidden:
the sun, the moon and the truth.

Buddha

However long the night, the dawn will break.
African Proverb

Truth is its own reward.
Plato

Truth, when not sought after, rarely comes to light.
Oliver Wendell Holmes

Do not anticipate trouble or worry about
what may happen. Keep in the sunlight.
Benjamin Franklin

The road to success is lined with many
tempting parking spaces.

Anon

An error can never become true however many
times you repeat it. The truth can never be
wrong, even if no one hears it.
Mohandas Karamchand Gandhi

The best way to destroy your enemy
is to make him your friend.

Abe Lincoln

There are only two mistakes one
can make along the road to truth;
not going all the way, and not starting.

Buddha

The greater danger for most men lies
not in setting our aim too high and falling short,
but in setting our aim too low
and achieving our mark.

Michelangelo

The greatest way to live with honor in this world
is to be what we pretend to be.

Socrates

We don't receive wisdom, we must discover it
for ourselves after a journey
that no one can take for us or spare us.

Marcel Proust

The future belongs to those who believe
in the beauty of their dreams.

Eleanor Roosevelt

To live is so startling
it leaves little time for anything else.

Emily Dickinson

Create the highest, grandest vision possible
for your life, because you become
what you believe.

Oprah Winfrey

Our greatest glory is not in never falling,
but in rising every time we fall.

Confucius

Courage doesn't always roar.
Sometimes courage is the quiet voice
at the end of the day saying,
"I will try again tomorrow."

Mary Anne Radmacher

A journey of a thousand miles
begins with a single step.

Lao-Tzu

Let your dreams bind your work to your play.

Bob Franke

The man who has no imagination has no wings.

Mohammed Ali

Happiness depends upon ourselves.

Aristotle

Man cannot discover new oceans unless
he has the courage to lose sight of the shore.

André Gide

The wisest mind has something yet to learn.

George Santayana

The price of wisdom is above rubies.

The Bible

Not a day passes over the earth but men
and women of no note do great deeds, speak
great words, and suffer noble sorrows. Of these
obscure heroes, philosophers and martyrs
the greater part will never be known.

Charles Reade

Be kind, for everyone you meet
is fighting a hard battle.

Plato

No man is wise enough by himself.

Titus Maccius Plautus

Wise sayings often fall on barren ground,
but a kind word is never thrown away.

Sir Arthur Helps

If you want others to be happy,
practice compassion.
If you want to be happy,
practice compassion.

Dalai Lama

A hundred times a day I remind myself that
my inner and outer life depends on
the labors of other men, living and dead,
and that I must exert myself in order to
give in the same measure as I have received
and am still receiving.

Albert Einstein

Trust men and they will be true to you;
treat them greatly and they
will show themselves great.

Ralph Waldo Emerson

Great people are those who make others
feel that they, too, can become great.

Mark Twain

Appreciation is a wonderful thing. It makes what
is excellent in others belong to us as well.

Voltaire

We make a living by what we get,
we make a life by what we give.

Sir Winston Churchill

The wisest men follow their own direction.

Euripides

Truth never damages a cause that is just.

Mohandas Karamchand Gandhi

Life grants nothing to us mortals
without hard work.

Horace

There is no power on earth more
formidable than the truth.

Margaret Lee Runbeck

Dignity exists not in possessing honors,
but in the consciousness
that we deserve them.

Aristotle

I know of no more encouraging fact
than the unquestioned ability of a man
to elevate his life by conscious endeavor.

Henry David Thoreau

Being defeated is often only a temporary condition.
Giving up is what makes it permanent.

Marilyn vos Savant

A wise man can see more
from the bottom of a well than a fool can
from a mountain top.

Anon

The definition of insanity is
doing the same thing over and over
and expecting different results.

Benjamin Franklin

I do not kow everything,
still many things I understand.

Johann Wolfgang von Goethe

Each day, and the living if it,
has to be a conscious creation in which
discipline and order are relieved with
some play and pure foolishness.

Mary Sarton

There are stars whose radiance is visible on earth
though they have long been extinct.
There are people whose brilliance continues
to light the world though
they are no longer among the living.
These lights are particularly bright
when the night is dark.

Hannah Senesh

You are not here merely to make a living.
You are here to enable the world
to live more amply, with greater vision,
and with a finer spirit of hope and achievement.
You are here to enrich the world.
You impoverish yourself
if you forget this errand.

Woodrow Wilson

I believe that to meet the challenge
of the next century, human beings will have to
develop a greater sense of universal responsibility.
Each of us must learn to work not just
for his or her own self, family or nation,
but for the benefit of all mankind.

Dalai Lama

All that is necessary for the forces of evil
to win in the world is for
enough good men to do nothing.

Edmund Burke

Who dares not speak his thoughts is a slave.

Euripides

Death is not the worst that can happen to men.

Plato

Freedom is from within.

Frank Lloyd Wright

Wise men, though all laws were abolished,
would live the same lives.

Aristophanes

If we were directed from Washington
when to sow and when to reap,
we would soon want bread.

Thomas Jefferson

If a man is called to be a street sweeper,
he should sweep streets even as Michelangelo
painted or Beethovan composed music
or Shakespeare wrote poetry.
He should sweep streets so well that all
the hosts of heaven and earth will pause and say,
"Here lived a great street sweeper
who did his job well."

Martin Luther King, Jr.

Let each man exercise the art he knows.

Aristophanes

Each man is the smith of his own fortune.

Appius Claudius Caecus

What we think we become.

Buddha.

A pessimist sees the difficulty
in every opportunity; an optimist sees
the opportunity in every difficulty.

Sir Winston Churchill

A sailor without a destination
cannot hope for a favorable wind.

Leon Tec

If you don't know where you're going,
you might not get there.

Yogi Berra

If you can dream it, you can do it.
Walt Disney

We will either find a way or make a way.
Hannibal

Anyone can hold the helm when the sea is calm.
Publilius Syrus

They are able because they think they are able.
Virgil

Have the courage to live. Anyone can die.
Robert Cody

A man who seeks truth and loves it must be
reckoned precious to any human society.

Frederick the Great

The price good men pay for indifference to public
affairs is to be ruled by evil men.

Plato

Our minds possess by nature an
insatiable desire to know the truth.

Cicero

To know that we know what we know,
and to know that we do not know
what we do not know,
that is true knowledge.

Copernicus

Nothing splendid has ever been achieved
except by those who dared believe
that something inside them
was superior to circumstance.

Bruce Barton

All truths are easy to understand once they are
discovered; the point is to discover them.

Galileo Galilei

Don't part with your illusions.
When they are gone you may still exist,
but you have ceased to live.

Mark Twain

Courage is not simply one of the virtues, but the
form of every virtue at the testing point.

C.S. Lewis

Truth is always the strongest argument.

Sophocles

We are not human beings on a spiritual journey.
We are spiritual beings on a human journey.

Steven Covey

Once you make a decision, the universe
conspires to make it happen.

Ralph Waldo Emerson

In the universe, great acts
are made up of small deeds.

Lao Tzu

Many persons have a wrong idea of what
constitutes true happiness. It is not attained
through self-gratification but through
fidelity to a worthy purpose.

Helen Keller

All people are a single nation.

Koran

If your actions inspire others to dream more,
learn more, do more and become more,
you are a leader.

John Qunicy Adams

If you see no reason for giving thanks,
the fault lies in yourself.

Native American Proverb
Minquass Tribe

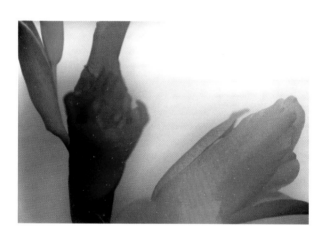

It is from numberless diverse acts of courage
and belief that human history is shaped.
Each time a man stands up for an ideal,
or acts to improve the lot of others,
or strikes out against injustice,
he sends forth a tiny ripple of hope.

Robert F. Kennedy

The significant problems we face
cannot be solved at the same level of thinking
with which we created them.

Albert Einstein

There is no end to the things you can accomplish.

Anon

To do for the world more than the
world does for you - that is success.

Henry Ford

Stay the course, light a star,
change the world where'ere you are.

Richard LeGallienne

A ship in the harbor is safe but
that's not what ships are built for.

William Thayer Shedd

Half the wrecks that strew the ocean,
if some star had been their guide,
might have now been riding safely
but they drifted with the tide.

Robert Whitacker

No pessimist ever discovered the secret of the stars,
or sailed to an uncharted land, or opened a new
doorway for the human spirit.

Helen Keller

As long as one keeps searching, the answers come.

Joan Baez

Your life is what your thoughts make it.

Marcus Aurelius

Turn your face to the sun and
the shadows fall behind you.

Maori Proverb

A man sooner or later discovers
that he is the master gardener of his soul,
the director of his life.

James Allen

Do not lost heart. The steeper the road,
the faster it rises toward ever wider horizons.

Popre John Pual II

Giving up is the ultimate tragedy.

Robert J. Donovan

There is no greater force than the force
of a man determined.

Anon

Smooth seas do no make skillful sailors.

African Proverb

Trust yourself. You know more
than you think you do.

Benjamin Spock

There are only two lasting bequests we can
hope to give our children.
One of these is roots; the other wings.

Hodding Carter

Use what talents you possess.
The woods would be very silent if no birds
sang there except those that sang best.

Henry Van Dyke

There are two ways to live your life.
One is as though nothing is a miracle.
The other is as though everything is.

Albert Einstein

Some people feel the rain.
Others just get wet.

Robert Zimmerman (Bob Dylan)

Stand often in the company of dreamers.
They believe you can achieve impossible things.

Mary Anne Radmacher

Let us not forget that the earth delights
to feel your bare feet and the winds
long to play with your hair.

Kahlil Gibran

A light heart lives long.

Shakespeare

And those who were seen dancing were thought
insane by those who could not hear the music.

Friedrich Wilhelm Nietzsche

To accomplish great things we must
dream as well as act.

Anatole France

I am not afriad of storms,
for I am learning to sail my ship.

Aeschylus

The wind that fills my sails propels,
but I am helmsman.

George Meredith

One ship drives east and the other drives west
While the self same breezes blow.
'Tis the set of the sails and not the gales
That determines the way they go.

Like the birds of the air are the ways of fate
As we journey along through life.
'Tis the set of the soul that determines the goal
And not the storm and the strife.

Ella Wheeler Wilcox